Chimpanzees

NorthWord Press
Chanhassen, Minnesota

DEDICATION
For Deb, Barry, and the Adventures of the Four Travelers
— D.D.

Photography © 2003: Anup Shah: cover, pp. 4, 5, 19, 22, 23, 28, 32-33, 42-43, back cover; Anup Shah/Dembinsky Photo Associates: pp. 6, 10, 17, 44; Kristin Mosher/Danita Delimont, Agent: pp. 8-9, 14-15, 36-37, 38-39, 41; Adam Jones: p. 13; Rob & Ann Simpson/Visuals Unlimited, Inc.: p. 16; Jenny Desmond: pp. 26-27; Gerry Ellis/Minden Pictures: p. 29; Stan Osolinski/Dembinsky Photo Associates: pp. 31, 34; Wendy Dennis/Dembinsky Photo Associates: p. 35.

Illustrations by John F. McGee
Designed by Russell S. Kuepper
Edited by Judy Gitenstein

NorthWord Press
18705 Lake Drive East
Chanhassen, MN 55317
1-800-328-3895
www.northwordpress.com

Library of Congress Cataloging-in-Publication Data

Dennard, Deborah.
    Chimpanzees / Deborah Dennard ; illustrations by John McGee.
        p.   cm.   – (Our wild world series)
    Summary: Discusses the physical characteristics, behavior, habitat, and life cycle of chimpanzees.
    ISBN 1-55971-846-3 (hc.) – ISBN 1-55971-845-5 (softcover)
    1. Chimpanzees—Juvenile literature. [1. Chimpanzees.] I. McGee, John F., ill. II. Title.
III. Series.

QL737.P96 D46 2003
599.885—dc21
                                                                    2002032646

Printed in Malaysia

10 9 8 7 6 5 4 3 2 1

Chimpanzees

Deborah Dennard
Illustrations by John F. McGee

NorthWord Press
Chanhassen, Minnesota

CHIMPANZEES are more like humans than just about any other animal. Scientists have studied chimpanzees, or chimps, as they are also known, very closely. Chimps and humans have similar social structures and behaviors. It is easy to look at chimpanzees and see something that is familiar.

Chimpanzees and humans are both primates (PRY-mates). One way to tell if an animal is a primate is to look at the hands and feet. A primate has 5 fingers on each hand and 5 toes on each foot. A primate has nails on the fingers and toes instead of claws. A primate also has opposable (uh-POE-zih-bull) thumbs.

This chimpanzee is using its opposable thumb to hold a thin plant stalk.

Baby chimpanzees, such as this one, seem to delight in playing with their elders.

Opposable thumbs and opposable big toes are needed for climbing trees.

Opposable thumbs can reach across the hand to touch all of the other fingers. An opposable thumb allows primates to grasp things. Humans use their thumbs to hold things such as pencils. Chimpanzees use them to hold branches, food, and many other things.

Chimps also have opposable big toes. Their big toes can reach across the foot to touch all the other toes. This makes both their thumbs and big toes excellent tools for holding and climbing.

Africa is home to all chimpanzees in the wild. Chimpanzees can live in many different habitats. A habitat may be a forest, a meadow, a desert, a rain forest, or any place where plants and animals live. Chimpanzees can live at sea level or 9,000 feet (2,730 meters) high in the eastern mountains.

The area in red shows where chimpanzees live in Africa.

Male chimpanzees weigh from about 95 pounds (43 kilograms) to about 110 pounds (50 kilograms). Males are about 3 feet (90 centimeters) tall. Females are smaller. They weigh about 70 pounds (30 kilograms) and average only about 2.5 feet (76 centimeters) tall.

All chimpanzees, both male and female, are strong and muscular. All chimpanzees have coarse (KORSE) black hair over most of their bodies. Some chimps have hairy faces. Some chimps have no hair on their faces. The skin of the face may be pink or dark gray or black.

Like all primates, chimpanzees have large heads in comparison to their bodies. This is because they have large brains and are very smart. Chimpanzees have large ears, heavy rounded eyebrow ridges, and flattened nostrils.

Male chimpanzees are large, powerful animals
with heavy, rounded eyebrow ridges.

Chimpanzees love to play. One of their favorite games is piggyback!

Chimpanzees have strong arms that are longer than their legs. Their arms and their legs are good for traveling on the ground or climbing in trees. When chimpanzees walk on the ground, they walk on their flat feet and on the knuckles of their curled hands. This is called knuckle walking. Chimps can walk very quickly in this way. They can also balance on their back legs and walk on just their feet, but this is less common and is much slower.

Chimps are a bit clumsy up in the trees. They do not travel as far or as long in the trees as they do on the ground.

Chimpanzees
FUNFACT:

As chimpanzees grow older their hair may turn gray. They may even become bald.

The scientific name for common chimpanzees is *Pan troglodytes*. Pan is the name of the Greek god of the forest who was part human and part animal. Troglodytes refers to cave men. So the scientific name suggests that chimpanzees are like people in some ways.

Common chimpanzees are great apes. Their closest relatives are gorillas and orangutans. All great apes belong to the same family, called the Pongid (PON-djid) family.

Both monkeys and apes are primates, but one difference is that monkeys have tails and apes do not.

Chimpanzees
FUNFACT:

There is a very rare species (SPEE-sees) of chimpanzee called the bonobo, or the pygmy (PIG-me) chimpanzee. It is smaller and darker than the common chimpanzee and lives only deep in the rain forests of the African Congo. There may be as few as 10,000 bonobos left in the world.

Bonobos are also known as pygmy chimpanzees.
They are smaller and rarer than common chimpanzees.

Chimpanzees live in groups called troops. They spend much time playing, touching, and grooming each other.

Chimpanzees live in groups, called communities or troops, that can be as large as 100. All of the members of the troop know each other, but sometimes smaller units within the troop team up to eat or travel or explore together. After a while, the smaller units join back up with the rest of the troop. Just like with people, some chimps like each other more and so spend more time sleeping, feeding, playing, and grooming together. It is almost as if chimpanzees have friends just like humans.

In each troop there may be chimps that are not as well liked as others. In fact, there are often animals in a troop that seem to actively dislike others. Sometimes one chimpanzee may even be bullied and chased by others. Usually, a troop is large enough that all of the animals can find other chimps to get along with.

Each chimp troop has male leaders. One of the most important things the leaders do is guide the troop and smaller units to search for food. In rain forests there is more food than in other places. Chimpanzees living in rain forests have smaller territories, or areas in which they find food, because they do not have to go far to gather all the food they need.

Food is harder to find in open woodlands and grasslands. Chimpanzees who live in these habitats have much larger territories, because they must travel farther in search of food. The territory of a troop may be about 20 square miles (52 square kilometers). Inside this territory individual chimps or units may claim a smaller area of their own. These individual territories may be only about 1.5 square miles (4 square kilometers). Chimps don't always stay in their own area. Sometimes they will explore the larger troop's territory, too.

Chimpanzees travel mainly on the ground, but they also climb high in trees to find fruit or to take a long look at their territory.

Chimpanzees are omnivores (OM-ni-vorz), which means that they eat both plants and meat. Chimpanzees have been known to eat more than 300 different kinds of food. They may eat as many as 20 different kinds of food in a day.

Fruit makes up about half of chimpanzees' plant diet. They love figs. When these sweet fruits are in season, chimps may eat very little else. When the season changes, the diet of the chimpanzees changes, too. They eat what is available. In addition to fruit, they eat honey, leaves, bark, and stems to round out their plant diet.

Meat is also an important part of the chimpanzees' diet. Termites are a favorite food and a good source of protein. Chimps also eat eggs, baby birds, and even small mammals such as monkeys. Meat is not eaten every day and is mostly hunted when plant food is harder to find.

Chimpanzees are omnivores and may eat as many as 300 different kinds of food, including plants and some meat.

One sign that chimps are highly intelligent animals is that they make and use tools. A tool is any object used in completing a task. Chimps use rocks as hammers to break open hard nuts. They pound open bee nests with heavy, club-like branches in their search for honey. They use pointed sticks to dig insect larvae (LAR-vee) from as far as two feet underground.

Chimpanzees also make tools to gather water. Thirsty chimpanzees spy water trapped deep in holes and crevices (KREV-iss-ez) of tree trunks. They grab a handful of leaves and chew them into a sponge-like mass. With their long fingers they wad up the chewed leaves and dip them in the hard-to-reach water. The leaves act like a sponge and soak up the water. Then the chimpanzee will squeeze the water from the leaves into its mouth.

Chimpanzees
FUNFACT:

It is believed that few animals other than humans and chimpanzees make tools.

Young chimpanzees learn how to use tools by watching adults and by playing with tools, such as this stick.

To catch termites, chimps select a stick or twig to use as a tool. They take off the leaves and sometimes the bark from the stick. Next they place the stick inside the small opening to the termite mound and wiggle the stick inside the mound a little bit. Then they wait patiently. After a few minutes the stick is slowly removed, inch by inch, from the termite mound. The tiny termites are hungrily licked off of the stick and eaten. Chimps use this same method to find and eat ants and bees.

A chimp uses a stick to fish for termites in a termite mound. Tiny termites clinging to the stick will be licked off and eaten.

Chimpanzees also go after larger prey (PRAY). They form hunting bands to stalk, corner, and catch prey such as colobus (COLL-uh-bus) monkeys, baboons, small antelope, and wild pigs. Chimps have the ability to communicate with each other and to work together to get things done. When they see a prey animal, a troop of male chimpanzees may turn into a fierce hunting band.

Different animals take on different jobs in the hunt. Some are blockers. They prevent the escape of the prey. Some are chasers. They race after the prey to send them into a trap of ambushers (AM-bush-ers). The ambushers are the ones who hide and wait for the prey. Then the ambushers rush in for the final kill.

All of the chimpanzees in the troop, male and female, young and old, watch the hunt. They hoot and scream in excitement. When the hunt is done, all of the members of the troop beg the hunters for the fresh meat.

Chimpanzees
FUNFACT:

As the chimpanzees hunt together they use many loud calls and hand signals that communicate to the other members of the hunting band what to do next.

Chimps love to tickle each other. They laugh, pant, and grin as they play.

Chimps spend a lot of time playing. They seem to enjoy being tickled. Mothers tickle their babies, and young and old chimpanzees tickle each other. They show their pleasure by opening their mouths into a playful grin, laughing a cackling laugh, and panting with delight.

Young chimpanzees learn the skills of being an adult chimpanzee through play. They roll stones or sticks or fruits on the ground and throw them high in the air and try to catch them. They play wild games of chase and tree climbing and tree swinging. This helps them gain the strength and coordination (ko-ord-ih-NAY-shun) they will need as adults. Other games include wrestling and a chimpanzee version of "Follow the Leader." This game often becomes a

These young chimpanzees are old enough to leave their mothers and play wild climbing and wrestling games together.

game of chase the leader! In games, young chimps learn who is strongest and smartest, and who will probably grow up to be leaders in the troop.

Playing can be seen in a chimpanzee troop at almost any time, except when it is raining. Chimps seem to dislike water and rain. They sometimes travel many miles out of their way to avoid crossing a river, even a small, shallow one. During rain they sit huddled together or find shelter in the trees. They do not eat or play or do anything except wait for it to stop raining.

Chimps make faces to communicate what they mean:
Playing (top left), frustration (top right), anger (bottom left), and fear (bottom right).

Chimpanzees communicate very well through calls, hoots, screams, and facial expressions (ex-PRESH-uns). Chimpanzees are very noisy. More than 30 calls and hoots have been identified by scientists. Most of these calls seem to have a specific meaning such as fear or alarm or comfort. By studying chimpanzee faces and behaviors, scientists have a good idea of what chimps are "saying" to each other. A grin of fear is a wide-open mouth with lips pulled tightly back to show teeth and gums. An angry face has lips that are pushed forward in a tight pout. Chimps show frustration by pushing their lips into an open-mouthed pout. Play is shown with a smile that may show teeth, but never teeth and gums. These same facial expressions can be seen on chimpanzees in the wild and on chimpanzees living in zoos.

Chimpanzees
FUNFACT:

When they see humans, chimpanzees usually bark out a short, sharp alarm call, then freeze in their tracks. Then, they may remain perfectly still or may try to disappear quietly into the brush.

Mother chimpanzees spend about 5 years caring for their babies.
This small baby is still very dependent on its mother.

Life in a chimpanzee troop is complex and always changing. Much of chimpanzee life is based on who will be leaders and who will be followers. Often this begins at birth.

Female chimpanzees become mature at about 8 years old. After that they have a baby about every 4 or 5 years. The mother devotes herself to caring for her baby for those 4 or 5 years and teaching it the many things it will need to know to be a strong adult.

A chimp baby starts life helpless and very small, weighing only about 3 pounds (1.5 kilograms). All members of the troop are curious about the new baby and want to have a look. It is the mother who decides whether her baby stays close to her or whether others are allowed a peek, or even to touch or cuddle with the baby.

Young babies cling to their mothers' bellies and nurse, or drink milk from their mothers' bodies. They nurse every hour for just a few minutes. As they grow larger they ride on their mothers' backs. They continue to nurse for nearly 5 years.

Riding on its mother's back is a good way for this young chimp to travel.

Soon, riding on mother's back is not only a good way to travel, it is another happy chimpanzee game. The baby may be brave enough to play with other chimps and go exploring or climbing. When it becomes frightened or unsure, it runs right back to its mother and hops on her back.

By age 3 the baby can eat solid food, climb, leap, and chase other young chimps. It also can travel out of its mother's reach. It may even go to other adult chimps and poke, prod, and pull hair. The adults ignore the play, and they simply walk away when they tire of the playful youngster.

By the time the baby is 4, the mother begins to wean the baby, or stop nursing, and make it more independent. She sometimes refuses the baby milk or a free ride on her back. Baby chimpanzees may become angry at this rejection. They might scream or kick. They might cry or throw rocks and sticks. This is the chimp version of a human baby having a temper tantrum! It may be hard for the mother to watch, but the mother knows she must teach her baby to grow up and away from her.

Chimpanzees
FUNFACT:

It takes about 240 days, or 8 months, for a baby chimpanzee to be born. It takes about 270 days, or 9 months, for a baby human to be born.

Baby chimpanzees have pink, hairless faces that turn darker and hairier as they grow older.

2

By about age 5 the babies are weaned and must feed themselves. Young chimps must keep up with the troop and eventually find a mate of their own. By this time the mother probably has a new baby. Throughout a chimp's life, though, it will spend some time with its mother now and then.

Young male chimpanzees form strong partnerships that are very much like friendships. They sometimes fight with each other, yet they know they must remain close and strong in order to protect the troop from being taken over by other male chimpanzees. Male chimps often stay in the troop into which they were born for their entire lives.

Usually every troop has a head male called the Alpha male. He is the strongest and the most willing to show how strong he is by hooting and screaming loudly. He walks around showing his strength by shaking branches. He looks even more frightening when the hairs on his body stand up on end. When the Alpha male displays like this, the other chimps in the troop show their respect for him. They may do this by backing away with their arms outstretched or by coming closer to groom him.

Chimpanzees
FUNFACT:

Chimps may spend hours cuddled together.
They pick through each others' fur, pat or even kiss each other,
and rest, a tangle of arms and legs and heads.

The male leader of a chimp troop is called the Alpha male.
He may scream and hoot and jump up and down to show his strength.

An older male leader, such as this one, may be challenged by a younger male for control of a chimpanzee troop.

Another male in the troop may challenge the Alpha male. If the challenger wins the fight, he may become the new leader of the troop, the new Alpha male.

Sometimes all of the adult males of a troop patrol the borders of their territory to make sure no other chimpanzee troops enter. If two troops meet at the edge of the territory, the meeting may be very noisy. The chimps may hoot and scream, slap the ground, or throw branches, leaves, and rocks in the air. Usually both troops back away into their own territories. Sometimes they fight, and that can be very bloody.

Chimps are strong and fast. They are not afraid to fight. When fighting, they use their long canine (KAY-nine) teeth and powerful molars and jaws to bite. They go out of their way to find heavy rocks and sticks to throw. When chimps "go to war" like this, they are making sure their territories are safe.

Chimpanzees can be very aggressive toward other animals. They are known to scream and hoot and throw rocks and sticks at possible predators (PRED-uh-torz) such as crocodiles, leopards, and snakes. This may scare the predators away.

Chimpanzees
FUNFACT:

Chimps in captivity or zoos have sometimes mistaken ropes and rubber hoses for snakes and have attacked them.

Two chimpanzees may throw rocks and sticks when they are fighting for control of territory or leadership of a troop.

At adulthood, female chimpanzees leave their birth troops. They wander about the savannah (suh-VAN-uh) or the forest in search of a new troop, a new place to call home. Females in a new troop may think the wandering female is an intruder and try to chase her away. Males in the new troop usually see the new female as a possible mate and welcome her. This can cause confusion.

It may take several months for a female to know whether or not she has been accepted into a new troop. Sometimes she may have to wander from troop to troop to find a new home. Once she is accepted by the new troop, she is a member for life.

This young chimpanzee will not have to worry about fighting to defend his troop until he is much older.

A chimpanzee troop's day begins shortly after dawn. When they wake up, they are hungry. Most of the morning is spent feeding and traveling to feeding spots. When the chimps find trees filled with fruit, they hoot and scream and pound on the tree trunks. They are calling the others to come share in the feast.

By noon the troop is tired and ready for a rest. Some chimps simply lie down on the ground to nap. Others climb into the trees or even build nests for naptime. Afternoon rest time lasts about 3 hours.

Sleeping is not the only activity that takes place during rest time. Chimpanzees need close physical contact. They touch and hold each other. This is called mutual (MEW-chu-ul) grooming. With mutual grooming, the chimps are clean and neat-looking and free of parasites (PAIR-uh-sites) and other unwanted pests. Mutual grooming means much more. Grooming is a way of keeping all of the members in the troop in close and peaceful contact. This is an important part of life for chimps.

Chimpanzees groom each other to stay clean and to keep the peace in the troop. Grooming is a way of saying, "All is well."

This mother of rare twin chimpanzees has twice as much work looking after both of her active babies.

By midafternoon the chimps continue in their search for food to try to fill their bellies before dark. This is the time when chimps may hunt for prey. Chimps might also look for termites or else just sit and eat figs and leaves. There is always some playing, too.

As dusk approaches, chimpanzees climb high into the trees and build a nest for the night. The higher the nest, the safer it is from predators. Nest building is a busy time. If the chimps are moving around in their territory, a new nest must be built every night. If the chimps are staying in the same spot, the same nest may be used again.

A chimp asleep in a nest.

To build a nest, a chimp selects a fork in a tree, a place where several strong branches meet. Branches are carefully bent over or broken and pulled in toward the center of the nest. The chimp may use its feet to hold larger branches in place while weaving smaller branches into the nest to hold it all together. If not enough branches and leaves are available, the chimp may leave the tree and gather leaves and branches elsewhere, bringing them back to the nest to finish it. Some nests are just a clump of messy leaves. Other nests are carefully woven, complex structures.

The best nest builders are adult female chimpanzees. They will let their babies of up to about 4 years old share their nests. Babies begin playing at nest building at about 1 year of age. By the time they must begin building their own nests at age 5, they are already good nest builders. Sometimes large male chimpanzees may watch a female build a nest and then chase her away and claim the nest for the night. The female does not object and simply moves on and builds a new nest.

Chimpanzees are at home in the trees or on the ground.
Chimps may find food or build nests in trees.

Young chimps in the wild grow stronger by climbing and playing together.

One hundred years ago there were probably as many as 5 million chimpanzees living in the woodlands and savannahs of central and west Africa. Now, in the beginning of the twenty-first century, that number may be down to 150,000. The number of chimpanzees becomes fewer every day.

Chimps have not always been treated well by humans. Chimpanzees in circuses or roadside zoos may be treated cruelly, fed poorly, and kept in small steel cages. Chimps kept as pets often are rejected when they are no longer little and cute.

Chimpanzees may remind us of ourselves. Only with the help of humans can they be saved from extinction.

Some humans hunt chimpanzees for meat or capture them to sell as illegal pets. The chimpanzees' greatest threat comes from the problem of too many people and not enough land for both chimps and people. As the forests, woodlands, and savannahs are turned into farms, pastures, parks, and towns, the chimpanzees lose their homes. Without a place to live, they cannot survive.

Chimpanzees are creatures with intelligence, with family ties, and with the ability to communicate and adapt to the world around them. Like people, they show a range of emotions, including fear, anger, frustration, and affection.

With a lot of care and help from humans in saving the homes of chimpanzees, these amazing animals will survive.

Chimpanzees
FUNFACT:

**A chimpanzee's life span is less than 50 years in the wild.
In captivity, some chimps have lived to be over 60.**

Internet Sites

You can find out more interesting information about chimpanzees and lots of other wildlife by visiting these Internet sites.

www.animal.discovery.com/	Animal Planet.com
www.animaltime.net/primates/	Aye-Aye's Primate Primer
www.chimphaven.org/gigi.htm	Chimp Haven
www.kidsplanet.org/	Defenders of Wildlife
www.enchantedlearning.com	Enchanted Learning.com
www.janegoodall.org	Jane Goodall Institute
www.lazoo.org/mahale.htm	Los Angeles Zoo
www.nationalgeographic.com/kids/creature_feature/0112/chimps.html	National Geographic Explorer for Kids
www.nwf.org/internationalwildlife/chimps.html	National Wildlife Federation
http://faculty.washington.edu/chudler/front.html	Neuroscience for Kids
www.oaklandzoo.org/atoz/azchimp.html	Oakland Zoo
www.pbs.org/wnet/nature/goodall/	PBS Nature Series
www.scz.org/animals/c/chimp.html	Sedgwick County Zoo
www.panda.org/kids/wildlife/mnchimp.htm	World Wildlife Fund

Index

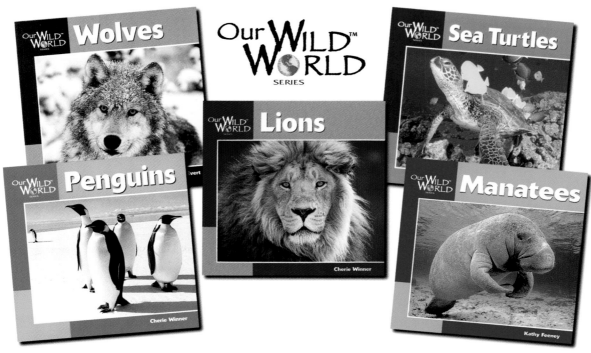

Titles available in the Our Wild World Series:

BISON
ISBN 1-55971-775-0

BLACK BEARS
ISBN 1-55971-742-4

CARIBOU
ISBN 1-55971-812-9

CHIMPANZEES
ISBN 1-55971-845-5

COUGARS
ISBN 1-55971-788-2

DOLPHINS
ISBN 1-55971-776-9

EAGLES
ISBN 1-55971-777-7

GORILLAS
ISBN 1-55971-843-9

LEOPARDS
ISBN 1-55971-796-3

LIONS
ISBN 1-55971-787-4

MANATEES
ISBN 1-55971-778-5

MONKEYS
ISBN 1-55971-849-8

MOOSE
ISBN 1-55971-744-0

ORANGUTANS
ISBN 1-55971-847-1

PENGUINS
ISBN 1-55971-810-2

POLAR BEARS
ISBN 1-55971-828-5

SEA TURTLES
ISBN 1-55971-746-7

SEALS
ISBN 1-55971-826-9

SHARKS
ISBN 1-55971-779-3

TIGERS
ISBN 1-55971-797-1

WHALES
ISBN 1-55971-780-7

WHITETAIL DEER
ISBN 1-55971-743-2

WOLVES
ISBN 1-55971-748-3

See your nearest bookseller, or order by phone 1-800-328-3895

NORTHWORD PRESS
Chanhassen, Minnesota